ITALY TRAVEL GUIDE 2023

Carl S. Robertson

Copyright 2023 by Carl Steves ROBERTSON

All rights reserved. No part of this publication may be reproduced, distributed, or transmitted in any form or by any means, including photocopying, recording, or other electronic or mechanical methods, without the prior written permission of the publisher, except in the case of brief quotations embodied in critical reviews and certain other non-commercial uses permitted by copyright law.

For permissions requests, please contact the publisher at carlrobertson@gmail.com

Disclaimer: The information provided in this book is for general informational purposes only. The author and publisher are not liable for any errors or omissions in the content or for any actions taken based on the information provided. The reader is solely responsible for their own choices and decisions.

TABLE OF CONTENTS

Table of Contents

TABLE OF CONTENTS 3

INTRODUCTION TO ITALY TRAVEL GUIDE 2023 4

....8

    1.1   Overview of Italy 9

    Geography and Climate 15

    1.2   History and Culture 19

Planning Your Trip to Italy 25

    2.1 Visa and Entry Requirements.............25

    2.2 Best Time to Visit Italy 29

    2.3 Packing Essentials 34

    2.4 Health and Safety Tips 39

    2.5 Currency and Money Matters.............46

Exploring the Regions of Italy 51

   3.1 Northern Italy(Milan, Venice, Lake Como)..51

   3.2 Central Italy (Rome,Florence, Tuscany) 57

   3.3 Southern Italy (Naples, Amalfi Coast, Sicily) 62

Must-See Attractions and Experiences 67

   4.1 Colosseum and Ancient Rome 67

   4.2 Vatican City and St. Peter's Basilica ..69

   4.3 The Duomo of Florence and Uffizi Gallery..71

   4.4 Italian Cuisine and Wine 73

   4.5 Outdoor Adventures and Nature Parks 77

....79

Practical Information and Tips 80

   5.1 Getting Around Italy 80

   5.2 Accommodation Options....................83

6.1 Essential Italian Phrases 91

6.2 Italian Alphabet and Pronunciation Guide
.... 95

Conclusion and Final Recommendations 98

BONUS 105

TRAVEL JOURNAL 105

INTRODUCTION TO ITALY TRAVEL GUIDE 2023

Once upon a time, there was a young adventurer named Emily who had always dreamed of exploring the enchanting landscapes and rich history of Italy. However, she had no idea where to start or how to plan her journey. Emily felt overwhelmed, unsure of how to turn her dream into reality.

One sunny day, while browsing through a local bookstore, Emily stumbled upon a book titled "Italy Travel Guide 2023." She picked it up, intrigued by the vibrant cover and the promise of unraveling the secrets of Italy. As she flipped through the pages, she realized that this book held the key to her dream.

Excitement filled her heart as she purchased the travel guide and rushed home. Sitting on her cozy couch, Emily delved into the pages, discovering a wealth of information about

Italy's regions, historical sites, and must-see attractions. Each chapter unfolded a new chapter of adventure waiting to be experienced.

With the Italy travel guide in hand, Emily began planning her journey. She found practical tips on obtaining a visa, choosing the best time to visit, and packing essentials tailored to each season. The guide also provided valuable insights into the local

customs and etiquette, ensuring she would respect the Italian way of life.

As she turned the pages, Emily's enthusiasm grew. She found detailed descriptions of the captivating cities of Milan, Rome, and Naples, along with their famous landmarks and hidden gems. The guide also pointed her towards the picturesque countryside of Tuscany and the breathtaking Amalfi Coast, urging her to explore beyond the well-trodden paths.

With a sense of direction and purpose, Emily meticulously crafted her itinerary, selecting the must-see attractions and experiences recommended by the guide. She marked the Colosseum, the Vatican, and the Leaning Tower of Pisa on her map, eagerly envisioning herself standing in awe before these iconic landmarks. She noted down the best places to sample authentic Italian cuisine, savoring the anticipation of indulging in delectable pasta, pizza, and gelato.

Armed with knowledge and inspiration from the Italy travel guide, Emily booked her flights and accommodations, ready to embark on her Italian adventure. The guide became her trusted companion throughout the journey, guiding her through the bustling streets of Rome, the picturesque canals of Venice, and the romantic alleys of Florence.

As Emily explored the wonders of Italy, she marveled at how the travel guide had transformed her journey. It had not only provided her with practical information but also ignited her curiosity and deepened her appreciation for Italy's rich culture and history. The stories and recommendations within the guide had unlocked a world of experiences she would have otherwise missed.

Throughout her trip, Emily met fellow travelers who, like her, had discovered their own path through the Italy travel guide. They exchanged stories, recommendations, and tips, each filled with gratitude for the invaluable resource that had transformed their journeys into unforgettable adventures.

By the end of her Italian odyssey, Emily realized that the Italy travel guide had been more than just a book—it had been her guiding light, illuminating her path and enriching her experiences. With a heart full of

1.1 Overview of Italy

Italy, located in Southern Europe, is a captivating country renowned for its rich history, stunning landscapes, vibrant culture, and delectable cuisine. With a population of over 60 million people, Italy is known for its diverse regions, each offering unique experiences and attractions.

Geographically, Italy is bordered by France, Switzerland, Austria, and Slovenia, with its distinct shape resembling a boot extending into the Mediterranean Sea. This strategic location has shaped Italy's history, making it a melting pot of civilizations and a crossroads of cultures.

Italy boasts a varied topography, encompassing majestic mountains, such as the Alps and the Apennines, picturesque coastal regions, and fertile plains. From the snow-capped peaks in the North to the sun-kissed beaches of the South, Italy's landscapes never fail to enchant visitors.

The country's rich history stretches back thousands of years, with influences from ancient civilizations such as the Etruscans, Romans, and Greeks. Italy is often referred to as the birthplace of Western civilization due to its significant contributions to art, architecture, literature, philosophy, and science.

Italy is renowned for its architectural wonders, including the iconic Colosseum in Rome, the majestic Duomo of Florence, and the grandeur of St. Mark's Basilica in Venice. The country is also home to countless historical sites and ruins, such as Pompeii, Herculaneum, and the Roman Forum, which provide a glimpse into the ancient world.

Italy's cultural heritage extends beyond its architectural marvels. It is a country that celebrates art, music, and fashion. From world-renowned art galleries like the Uffizi in Florence to opera performances at La Scala in Milan, Italy offers a feast for the senses.

One cannot discuss Italy without mentioning its culinary prowess. Italian cuisine is celebrated worldwide for its simplicity, fresh ingredients, and mouthwatering flavors. From traditional pasta dishes like spaghetti alla carbonara to Neapolitan pizzas and creamy gelato, Italy offers a gastronomic adventure like no other.

The regions of Italy each have their distinct characteristics and attractions. The bustling capital city of Rome is home to ancient ruins and religious landmarks, while Florence showcases Renaissance masterpieces and Tuscan charm. The romantic canals of Venice and the glamorous coastline of the Amalfi Coast add to Italy's allure.

Italy's natural beauty is equally captivating. The country is blessed with stunning lakes, such as Lake Como and Lake Garda, picturesque coastal areas like the Cinque Terre, and breathtaking islands such as Sicily and Sardinia. The rolling vineyards of Tuscany and the rugged landscapes of the Dolomites provide opportunities for outdoor adventures and exploration.

Italians take pride in their warm hospitality and zest for life. They embrace the "dolce vita" lifestyle, appreciating the finer things in life, cherishing time spent with family and friends, and relishing in simple pleasures.

In summary, Italy is a country that seamlessly blends ancient history with modern charm, captivating visitors with its cultural treasures, natural wonders, and culinary delights. Whether exploring the iconic landmarks of Rome, getting lost in the labyrinthine streets of Venice, or indulging in the art and culture of Florence, Italy offers a journey that will leave a lasting impression on every traveler.

Geography and Climate

Italy, located in Southern Europe, is a diverse and captivating country known for its stunning landscapes and historical significance. Its geographical features contribute to a varied climate throughout different regions, offering a wide range of experiences for travelers. Understanding the geography and climate of Italy is essential for planning a successful and enjoyable trip.

Geographically, Italy is situated on the Italian Peninsula, which extends into the Mediterranean Sea. It shares land borders with several countries, including France, Switzerland, Austria, and Slovenia. The peninsula is shaped like a boot, with its southern tip reaching towards the island of Sicily. Italy is also home to two major Mediterranean islands, Sardinia and Sicily, along with numerous smaller islands scattered along its coastline.

The Apennine Mountains, which run from the northwest to the southern part of Italy, form the country's backbone. These mountains divide the country into distinct regions, each with its own unique landscape and cultural identity. Northern Italy is characterized by the stunning Italian Alps, including the Dolomites, offering breathtaking mountain scenery and excellent opportunities for outdoor activities such as hiking, skiing, and mountaineering. Central Italy is known for its rolling hills, fertile plains, and picturesque vineyards, while the south boasts rugged coastlines, picturesque islands, and volcanic landscapes.

Italy's geography also blesses it with a diverse climate. In general, Italy has a Mediterranean climate, characterized by hot summers and mild, wet winters. However, due to the country's varied topography, there are regional variations in climate. The northern regions, including Lombardy and Veneto, experience cold winters and hot summers. The Alps in the north receive heavy snowfall, making them popular destinations for winter sports enthusiasts.

Central Italy, encompassing Tuscany, Umbria, and Lazio, enjoys a milder climate. Summers are warm and dry, while winters are relatively mild and wet. This region is known for its rolling countryside, vineyards, and historic cities like Florence and Rome.

Southern Italy and the islands have a Mediterranean climate with hot, dry summers and mild, rainy winters. The southernmost regions, such as Calabria and Sicily, benefit from longer summers and milder winters due to their proximity to North Africa. The southern coastlines, including the Amalfi Coast and the islands of Capri and Sicily, are renowned for their picturesque beauty and pleasant climate.

It's important to consider the climate when planning your visit to Italy. The summer months, from June to August, are the peak tourist season, especially in coastal areas. Spring (April to May) and autumn (September to October) offer pleasant temperatures and fewer crowds, making them ideal for exploring cities and countryside. Winter (November to February) is a quieter time with lower prices, particularly in the northern regions where you can enjoy winter sports.

In conclusion, Italy's geography and climate contribute to its remarkable diversity and offer a range of experiences for travelers. From the snow-capped peaks of the Alps to the sun-soaked beaches of the Mediterranean, Italy's landscapes and climate vary greatly across its regions. Understanding these geographical and climatic nuances will help you plan your itinerary and make the most of your journey through this enchanting country.

1.2 History and Culture

Italy, known as the birthplace of Western civilization, boasts a captivating history and a rich cultural heritage that spans thousands of years. From the ancient Roman Empire to the Renaissance period and beyond, the country's historical and cultural contributions have left an indelible mark on the world. This section provides a comprehensive overview of Italy's history and culture, offering insights into its significant milestones, artistic achievements, and cultural traditions.

1.3.1 Ancient Italy:

Italy's history can be traced back to ancient times when it was home to various civilizations and tribes. The Etruscans, Greeks, and Romans all played pivotal roles in shaping the region's early history. The Romans, in particular, established a vast empire that stretched across Europe, North Africa, and the Middle East, leaving behind remarkable architectural structures, such as the Colosseum and the Forum in Rome.

1.3.2 The Renaissance and Artistic Legacy:

The Renaissance period, which flourished in Italy between the 14th and 17th centuries, marked a significant cultural and intellectual revival. Italian cities such as Florence,

Venice, and Rome became vibrant centers of art, literature, and scientific advancements. Renowned artists like Leonardo da Vinci, Michelangelo, and Raphael created masterpieces that continue to inspire awe and admiration to this day. The Italian Renaissance not only revolutionized the arts but also influenced philosophy, politics, and the sciences.

1.3.3 Italian Cuisine and Gastronomy:

Italian cuisine is renowned worldwide for its delicious flavors and regional diversity. From pasta and pizza to gelato and espresso, Italy offers a gastronomic experience that is unparalleled. Each region has its culinary specialties, with dishes like Neapolitan pizza, Tuscan ribollita, and Sicilian cannoli showcasing the diverse flavors and traditions of Italian cooking. Exploring Italy's culinary landscape is an integral part of experiencing its culture.

1.3.4 Festivals and Traditions:

Italians are known for their vibrant celebrations and deeply rooted traditions. Throughout the year, numerous festivals and events take place, providing an opportunity to witness the country's cultural richness. The Venice Carnival, the Palio di Siena, and the Infiorata in Spello are just a few examples of the colorful and festive traditions that reflect Italy's deep sense of community and pride.

1.3.5 Architecture and Landmarks:

Italy's architectural heritage is awe-inspiring, with iconic landmarks and structures scattered throughout the country. From the architectural grandeur of ancient Rome to the breathtaking cathedrals, palaces, and piazzas, Italy offers a visual feast for history and art enthusiasts alike. The architectural marvels of Florence's Duomo, the intricate mosaics of Ravenna's churches, and the picturesque beauty of the Cinque Terre coastal villages are just a glimpse into Italy's architectural wonders.

1.3.6 Language and Literature:

The Italian language, derived from Latin, holds a prominent place in the country's cultural identity. Italy has produced world-renowned literary figures, such as Dante Alighieri, Petrarch, and Giovanni Boccaccio, who played pivotal roles in shaping European literature during the Middle Ages. Italian literature encompasses various genres, including poetry, epic narratives, and plays, capturing the essence of Italian culture and language.

1.3.7 Music and Opera:

Italy's contributions to classical music and opera are significant. Composers like Verdi, Puccini, and Rossini have created timeless operatic masterpieces that continue to be performed on renowned stages worldwide. Italian music extends beyond the realm of opera, with traditional folk music, classical compositions, and modern pop and rock genres enriching the country's musical landscape.

Planning Your Trip to Italy

2.1 Visa and Entry Requirements

When planning a trip to Italy, it is essential to understand the visa and entry requirements to ensure a smooth and hassle-free journey. The following comprehensive guide will provide you with the necessary information to navigate the process effectively.

Passport Validity:

Before traveling to Italy, ensure that your passport is valid for at least six months beyond your planned departure date. It is advisable to check your passport's expiration date and renew it if necessary.

Schengen Visa:

Italy is a part of the Schengen Area, which is a group of 26 European countries that have abolished passport control at their mutual borders. If you are a citizen of a country that is not part of the Schengen Area, you will likely need to apply for a Schengen Visa to enter Italy.

Check with the Italian embassy or consulate in your home country to determine the specific visa requirements and procedures. The application process usually involves submitting the required documentation, such as a completed application form, passport-sized photos, a valid passport, proof of travel insurance, and proof of accommodation and itinerary.

Visa-Free Travel:

Citizens of certain countries may be exempt from obtaining a Schengen Visa for short visits to Italy. These countries include the United States, Canada, Australia, New Zealand, and many others. However, it is crucial to check the latest visa regulations and requirements, as they may change periodically.

Generally, visa-free travelers are allowed to stay in Italy and the Schengen Area for up to 90 days within a 180-day period for tourism, business, or family visits.

Long-Term Stay and Residence Permits:

If you plan to stay in Italy for more than 90 days or have intentions beyond tourism, such as studying, working, or joining family members, you will need to apply for a long-term stay visa or a residence permit.

These permits require additional documentation, such as proof of accommodation, proof of financial means, health insurance, and specific application forms. The process can vary depending on the purpose of your stay, so it is crucial to consult the Italian embassy or consulate in your home country for accurate and up-to-date information.

Entry Requirements:

Upon arrival in Italy, you may be required to present certain documents to immigration authorities. These typically include a valid passport, proof of sufficient funds to cover your stay, proof of onward or return travel, and accommodation details.

It is advisable to carry copies of your travel insurance, visa, and other important documents in case they are requested by immigration officials. Additionally, ensure that your passport is stamped upon entry to comply with the necessary regulations.

COVID-19 Travel Restrictions:

Due to the global COVID-19 pandemic, travel restrictions and entry requirements may be in place. It is crucial to stay informed about the latest guidelines and regulations imposed by the Italian government and health authorities.

Check the official websites of the Italian Ministry of Foreign Affairs and the Italian Embassy or Consulate in your home country for the most up-to-date information on travel restrictions, testing requirements, and any quarantine measures.

It is important to note that visa and entry requirements can vary depending on your nationality and the purpose of your visit. Therefore, it is recommended to consult the official websites of the Italian government or seek advice from the Italian embassy or consulate in your home country for the most accurate and updated information specific to your situation.

By familiarizing yourself with the visa and entry requirements, you can ensure a smooth and stress-free journey to Italy, allowing you to fully immerse yourself in the country's rich culture, history, and breathtaking landscapes.

2.2 Best Time to Visit Italy

Italy is a country blessed with diverse landscapes, rich history, and vibrant culture.

The best time to visit Italy largely depends on your preferences, the regions you wish to explore, and the experiences you seek. Each season offers its own unique charm and highlights, allowing visitors to tailor their trip based on their desired activities and weather preferences. Here is a comprehensive guide to help you determine the best time to visit Italy:

Spring (March to May):

Spring is a delightful time to visit Italy as the weather starts to warm up, and the landscapes come alive with blooming flowers and lush greenery. The temperatures are generally mild, making it perfect for exploring cities and enjoying outdoor activities. However, do note that popular tourist destinations can be crowded during Easter week, especially in cities like Rome and Florence.

Summer (June to August):

Summer in Italy is synonymous with long, sunny days and bustling tourist activity. The weather is warm to hot, especially in the southern regions and coastal areas. This is an ideal time to visit if you plan to relax on Italy's stunning beaches, enjoy outdoor festivals, and indulge in al fresco dining. It's worth noting that popular tourist destinations like Rome, Venice, and the Amalfi Coast can be crowded during peak summer months.

Fall (September to November):

Fall brings cooler temperatures and fewer crowds, making it an excellent time to explore Italy's cultural treasures. The landscapes transform into a tapestry of vibrant autumn colors, particularly in regions like Tuscany and Umbria. September is still relatively warm, while November tends to be cooler and more rainy. This season is perfect for wine enthusiasts, as it coincides with the grape harvest and offers opportunities to participate in wine festivals and tastings.

Winter (December to February):

Italy experiences milder winters compared to some other European countries, making it an attractive destination for winter travel. While the northern regions and mountainous areas receive snowfall and offer skiing opportunities, the central and southern parts of Italy experience milder temperatures. Winter is an ideal time to visit cities like Rome, Florence, and Venice, as they are less crowded, and you can explore the famous landmarks without the usual throngs of tourists. Additionally, the holiday season in December brings festive markets and decorations, creating a magical atmosphere.

Shoulder Seasons:

The shoulder seasons of spring (March to May) and fall (September to November) are considered favorable times to visit Italy. During these periods, you can enjoy pleasant weather, fewer crowds, and potentially lower prices on accommodations and flights. It's an opportune time to explore popular tourist destinations at a more relaxed pace and immerse yourself in the local culture.

When planning your trip, also consider any specific events or festivals you may want to experience. Italy is renowned for its festivals, such as Venice Carnival in February, Easter processions in various cities, the Palio horse race in Siena in July and August, and the opera season at Verona Arena during the summer months.

Ultimately, the best time to visit Italy depends on your personal preferences and the experiences you seek. Whether you desire vibrant city life, beach relaxation, cultural exploration, or culinary adventures, Italy offers something to captivate every traveler, no matter the season.

2.3 Packing Essentials

When preparing for your trip to Italy, it is crucial to pack smart and efficiently. Having the right essentials in your luggage will ensure that you are well-prepared for various weather conditions, cultural expectations, and the activities you plan to engage in. Here is a comprehensive list of packing essentials for your journey to Italy:

Clothing:

Lightweight and breathable clothing: Pack comfortable and lightweight outfits suitable for the Mediterranean climate. Opt for breathable fabrics such as cotton or linen to keep cool during the warm summer months.

Sweaters or light jackets: Evenings can get cooler, especially in spring and autumn, so pack a couple of sweaters or light jackets for layering.

Modest attire for visiting religious sites: Remember to pack modest clothing that covers shoulders and knees for visits to churches and religious sites.

Comfortable walking shoes: Italy's cobblestone streets require comfortable footwear. Pack a pair of sturdy walking shoes or sneakers for exploring the cities and historical sites. If planning to hike or trek, include a pair of hiking boots or sturdy trail shoes.

Swimwear: If your itinerary includes coastal areas or hotel pools, pack swimwear for a refreshing dip in the Mediterranean.

Travel Documents:

Passport: Ensure your passport is valid for at least six months beyond your planned departure date.

Visa: Check the visa requirements based on your nationality and ensure you have obtained the necessary visa prior to your trip.

Travel insurance: Consider purchasing travel insurance to protect yourself against unforeseen circumstances, such as medical emergencies or trip cancellations.

Photocopies and digital copies: Carry photocopies or digital copies of your passport, visa, travel insurance, and other important documents. Store them separately from the originals.

Electronics:

Universal power adapter: Italy uses European-style power outlets, so bring a universal power adapter to charge your electronic devices.

Mobile phone and charger: Stay connected by bringing your mobile phone and charger. Check with your service provider about international roaming plans or consider purchasing a local SIM card.

Camera: Capture the beauty of Italy with a camera or smartphone equipped with a good camera. Don't forget extra memory cards and charging cables.

Personal Care Items:

Toiletries: Pack travel-sized toiletries, including toothpaste, toothbrush, shampoo, conditioner, soap, and any specific personal care items you require.

Medications: If you take prescription medications, ensure you have an ample supply for the duration of your trip. Carry them in their original packaging, along with any necessary prescriptions.

First aid kit: It's always a good idea to have a basic first aid kit with band-aids, pain relievers, antihistamines, and any other personal medications or supplies you may need.

Travel guidebook: Consider carrying a compact travel guidebook or download a digital version to have valuable information and recommendations at your fingertips.

Money and cards: Carry a mix of cash and cards for your financial needs. Notify your bank and credit card companies about your travel plans to avoid any issues with transactions.

Remember to pack light and be mindful of luggage weight restrictions, especially if planning to use budget airlines or public transportation. Packing efficiently will allow you to move around more comfortably and make room for souvenirs along the way.

As you prepare for your adventure in Italy, customize this list according to your personal needs and preferences. With the right essentials, you'll be ready to immerse yourself in the beauty, history, and culture that Italy has to offer.

2.4 Health and Safety Tips

2.4 Health and Safety Tips

When traveling to Italy, it's important to prioritize your health and safety to ensure a smooth and enjoyable trip. By following these health and safety tips, you can minimize potential risks and focus on creating unforgettable memories:

Travel Insurance: Before embarking on your journey, ensure that you have comprehensive travel insurance that covers medical emergencies, trip cancellations, and lost belongings. Familiarize yourself with the policy coverage and keep a copy of the insurance details with you at all times.

Medical Preparations:

Consult your healthcare provider: Schedule a visit to your doctor or a travel health clinic at least 4-6 weeks before your departure to discuss any necessary vaccinations, medication, or health advice specific to your needs.

Pack a first aid kit: Include essential items such as prescription medications, over-the-counter medications (pain relievers, anti-diarrheal, antihistamines), band-aids, antiseptic wipes, and any personal medical supplies.

Emergency Numbers: Save important phone numbers in your mobile phone or write them down in case of emergencies. This includes local emergency services, your travel insurance company, embassy or consulate contact information, and your designated emergency contact back home.

Stay Hydrated and Practice Good Hygiene:

Drink bottled water: While tap water is generally safe in most parts of Italy, it's advisable to drink bottled water to avoid any potential stomach upsets.

Hand hygiene: Wash your hands frequently with soap and water, especially before eating or after using public facilities. Carry a hand sanitizer with you for times when soap and water are not readily available.

Food and Water Safety:

Choose reputable establishments: Opt for restaurants and food vendors with good hygiene practices and high turnover of customers.

Safe food practices: Ensure that meat, seafood, and eggs are thoroughly cooked. Avoid consuming raw or undercooked food, including salads, unless you are certain of the cleanliness and quality of the ingredients.

Water precautions: If you prefer drinking tap water, confirm with the locals if it is safe in the specific region you are visiting. Otherwise, rely on bottled water for drinking and brushing your teeth.

Sun Protection:

Sunscreen: Protect your skin from harmful UV rays by applying sunscreen with a high SPF before going outdoors. Reapply frequently, especially after swimming or sweating.

Hats and sunglasses: Wear a wide-brimmed hat and sunglasses to shield your face and eyes from direct sunlight.

Seek shade: During peak sun hours (usually between 10 am and 4 pm), seek shade or take breaks indoors to minimize sun exposure.

Personal Safety:

Stay vigilant: Be aware of your surroundings, especially in crowded tourist areas, and keep an eye on your belongings to prevent theft or pickpocketing.

Use secure transportation: Choose licensed taxis or reputable car rental services. If using public transportation, be cautious of your belongings and avoid isolated or poorly lit areas, especially at night.

Emergency exits: Familiarize yourself with the emergency exits and safety procedures of your accommodation, as well as any attractions or venues you visit.

Local Laws and Customs:

Research local laws and customs before your trip to ensure you respect and abide by them. Familiarize yourself with appropriate dress codes for religious sites and cultural sensitivities in different regions of Italy.

COVID-19 Precautions:

Stay updated on travel advisories and COVID-19 protocols issued by health authorities and the Italian government. Follow guidelines such as wearing masks, practicing physical distancing, and frequent handwashing.

Check entry requirements: Confirm if Italy has any specific entry requirements, such as presenting proof of vaccination or negative COVID

2.5 Currency and Money Matters

When planning your trip to Italy, it's important to familiarize yourself with the currency and money matters to ensure a smooth financial experience during your travels. Here are some comprehensive guidelines to help you navigate currency exchange, payment options, and managing your money effectively in Italy.

Currency:

The official currency of Italy is the Euro (€). It is denoted by the symbol "€" and is divided into cents (1 Euro = 100 cents).

Ensure that you have some Euro notes and coins with you before arriving in Italy to cover immediate expenses such as transportation or small purchases upon arrival.

Currency Exchange:

You can exchange your currency to Euros at various places in Italy, including banks, currency exchange offices, and some hotels. Banks often offer competitive exchange rates, but they may charge a transaction fee.

It's advisable to avoid exchanging currency at airports or touristy areas, as they generally offer less favorable rates and higher fees.

Before exchanging your currency, compare rates and fees among different exchange services to find the best deal.

Keep in mind that it's always a good idea to have a mix of cash and alternative payment methods for flexibility.

ATMs and Cash Withdrawals:

ATMs (Automated Teller Machines) are widely available in Italy, even in smaller towns. They provide a convenient way to withdraw cash in Euros using your debit or credit card.

Check with your bank or card issuer regarding any international fees for ATM withdrawals or foreign currency transactions. Notify them of your travel plans to ensure your card is authorized for use in Italy.

Look for ATMs affiliated with major banks to ensure security and reasonable exchange rates. Be cautious of standalone ATMs in less crowded areas, as they may have higher fees or security risks.

Credit Cards and Debit Cards:

Credit and debit cards are widely accepted in most establishments in Italy, including hotels, restaurants, shops, and tourist attractions. Visa and Mastercard are the most commonly accepted cards, followed by American Express and Discover, which may have more limited acceptance.

Notify your card issuer about your travel plans to avoid any unexpected card blocks due to suspected fraudulent activity.

Keep in mind that some smaller establishments, especially in rural areas, may only accept cash. It's always a good idea to carry some cash as a backup.

Payment Options:

In addition to cash and cards, mobile payment options like Apple Pay, Google Pay, and Samsung Pay are increasingly accepted in larger cities and popular tourist destinations. Ensure that your mobile payment app is set up and linked to a valid payment method before your trip.

Traveler's checks are not widely accepted in Italy and may be difficult to exchange. It's recommended to rely on other payment methods mentioned above.

Budgeting and Expenses:

Italy, especially major cities like Rome, Florence, and Venice, can be relatively expensive. Plan your budget accordingly, considering accommodation, meals, transportation, sightseeing, and shopping expenses.

Research and make reservations in advance for accommodations and attractions to secure better prices and avoid last-minute surcharges.

Take note of any additional charges or fees associated with attractions, such as museum entrance fees or guided tour costs. These expenses can add up, so factor them into your budget.

Safety and Security:

While Italy is generally a safe country, it's important to take precautions to protect your money and valuables. Avoid carrying large amounts of cash and keep an eye on your belongings, especially in crowded areas and public transportation.

Use hotel safes to store your passports, spare cash, and other valuables. Consider carrying a money belt or a secure travel wallet.

Exploring the Regions of Italy

3.1 Northern Italy(Milan, Venice, Lake Como)

Northern Italy is a region known for its rich cultural heritage, stunning architecture, and breathtaking landscapes. It encompasses vibrant cities like Milan and Venice, as well as the tranquil beauty of Lake Como. Each destination offers a unique experience, combining historical significance, artistic treasures, and natural wonders.

3.1.1 Milan:

Milan, the fashion and financial capital of Italy, is a bustling metropolis that seamlessly blends modernity with historical charm. The city is famous for its iconic Duomo di Milano, a magnificent Gothic cathedral that dominates the city skyline. Visitors can explore the interior of the cathedral, ascend to the rooftop for panoramic views, and marvel at its intricate architecture.

Milan is also renowned for its world-class museums and art galleries. The Pinacoteca di Brera houses a vast collection of Italian Renaissance art, including masterpieces by renowned artists like Raphael and Caravaggio. The Leonardo da Vinci National Museum of Science and Technology is a must-visit, showcasing the genius of the legendary inventor.

Fashion enthusiasts will find their haven in Milan's Quadrilatero della Moda, a district filled with luxury boutiques and designer shops. The city comes alive during Milan Fashion Week, where the latest trends grace the runways and fashion enthusiasts flock to witness the glamour firsthand.

3.1.2 Venice:

Venice, a city built on a lagoon, is a true marvel. Its intricate network of canals, elegant bridges, and stunning architecture make it one of the most romantic and unique destinations in the world. Explore the iconic St. Mark's Square, home to the stunning St. Mark's Basilica and the Doge's Palace, which showcases Venetian Gothic architecture.

No visit to Venice is complete without a gondola ride along the narrow canals. Drift through the waterways, passing under picturesque bridges and admiring the enchanting buildings that line the canals. Discover the charming neighborhoods of San Marco, Cannaregio, and Dorsoduro, each offering their own distinct character and hidden gems.

Venice is also famous for its art, hosting the Biennale, one of the world's most prestigious contemporary art exhibitions. The city is dotted with art galleries and museums, including the Gallerie dell'Accademia, which houses an impressive collection of Venetian Renaissance art.

3.1.3 Lake Como:

Nestled amidst the foothills of the Alps, Lake Como is a natural paradise renowned for its serene beauty. The crystal-clear waters of the lake are surrounded by charming villages, opulent villas, and lush gardens. Take a leisurely boat ride across the lake to explore the idyllic towns of Bellagio, Varenna, and Menaggio, each offering stunning views and a relaxed atmosphere.

Visit Villa del Balbianello, a picturesque villa located on the lake's edge and surrounded by impeccably manicured gardens. This magnificent villa has been featured in several films, including James Bond's "Casino Royale."

Nature lovers can embark on hikes or bike rides through the surrounding hills and enjoy panoramic vistas of the lake and the surrounding landscapes. The region is also known for its scenic hiking trails, such as the

Greenway del Lago di Como, which winds its way along the lake's shore.

In conclusion, Northern Italy, encompassing Milan, Venice, and Lake Como, offers a captivating blend of art, history, and natural beauty. Whether strolling through Milan's fashionable streets, gliding along Venice's canals, or admiring the serene vistas of Lake Como, visitors are sure to be enchanted by the diverse and captivating experiences this region has to offer.

3.2 Central Italy (Rome, Florence, Tuscany)

Central Italy is a region that captivates travelers with its rich history, cultural heritage, and breathtaking landscapes. This chapter explores the enchanting cities of Rome and Florence, along with the picturesque region of Tuscany, offering a glimpse into the wonders that await visitors.

3.2.1 Rome:

Known as the "Eternal City," Rome is a treasure trove of ancient ruins, majestic monuments, and vibrant street life. From the iconic Colosseum to the awe-inspiring Vatican City, Rome is a testament to the grandeur of the Roman Empire and the seat of the Catholic Church.

Colosseum: Standing as a symbol of ancient Rome's power and architectural prowess, the Colosseum is a must-visit landmark. Step back in time as you explore its amphitheater and imagine the spectacles that unfolded within its walls.

Vatican City: Embark on a journey to the world's smallest independent state, home to St. Peter's Basilica and the Vatican Museums. Marvel at Michelangelo's masterpiece, the Sistine Chapel, and discover the rich artistic and cultural heritage preserved within these sacred walls.

Roman Forum: Roam through the remnants of ancient Rome's political, social, and economic hub. Explore the ruins of temples, basilicas, and arches, immersing yourself in the city's vibrant past.

Trevi Fountain: Toss a coin into the legendary Trevi Fountain to ensure your return to Rome.

Admire the intricate sculptures and indulge in the charm of this iconic Baroque masterpiece.

3.2.2 Florence:

Renowned as the birthplace of the Renaissance, Florence is a city that exudes art, culture, and architectural marvels. From world-class museums to breathtaking cathedrals, Florence offers a feast for the senses.

The Duomo of Florence: Gaze in awe at the magnificent Florence Cathedral, also known as the Duomo, with its stunning dome designed by Brunelleschi. Climb to the top for panoramic views of the city.

Uffizi Gallery: Delve into the world of art at the Uffizi Gallery, home to an extensive collection of Renaissance masterpieces. Admire works by Botticelli, Michelangelo, and Leonardo da Vinci, among others.

Ponte Vecchio: Cross the iconic Ponte Vecchio, a medieval bridge lined with jewelry shops that spans the Arno River. Enjoy the enchanting views and explore the artisan boutiques.

Piazza della Signoria: Immerse yourself in the heart of Florence's political and social life at Piazza della Signoria. Marvel at the Palazzo Vecchio, adorned with stunning sculptures, and soak up the vibrant atmosphere of this historical square.

3.2.3 Tuscany:

Just beyond Florence lies the picturesque region of Tuscany, renowned for its rolling hills, vineyards, and charming medieval towns. Tuscany offers a serene escape and an opportunity to indulge in world-class wine and gastronomy.

Siena: Discover the medieval charm of Siena, with its stunning cathedral and the famous

Piazza del Campo, where the thrilling Palio horse race takes place. Explore the narrow streets and enjoy the city's warm atmosphere.

San Gimignano: Journey to the hilltop town of San Gimignano, known for its well-preserved medieval architecture and iconic towers. Explore the narrow lanes, visit the local artisan shops, and savor the town's renowned gelato.

Chianti Wine Region: Embark on a wine-tasting adventure in the scenic Chianti region. Visit vineyards and wineries, sample world-class wines, and savor the flavors of the region's

3.3 Southern Italy (Naples, Amalfi Coast, Sicily)

Southern Italy is a region that captivates visitors with its breathtaking landscapes, historical sites, and vibrant culture. Within this region, three standout destinations beckon travelers: Naples, the Amalfi Coast, and Sicily. Each of these places offers a unique experience, filled with charm, history, and natural beauty.

3.3.1 Naples:

Naples, the bustling capital of the Campania region, is a city steeped in history and culinary delights. Known for its vibrant atmosphere and lively streets, Naples offers a glimpse into authentic Italian life. Visitors can explore the historic center, a UNESCO World Heritage Site, and wander through narrow alleys, uncovering hidden churches, colorful markets, and vibrant piazzas. Don't miss the chance to sample the city's iconic pizza, considered the birthplace of this beloved dish. Naples is also a gateway to nearby attractions like the ruins of Pompeii and Mount Vesuvius.

3.3.2 Amalfi Coast:

Stretching along the picturesque coastline of the Sorrentine Peninsula, the Amalfi Coast is a dream destination for nature lovers and romantics alike. The region is renowned for its dramatic cliffs, pastel-colored fishing villages, and crystal-clear turquoise waters. The town of Amalfi, with its medieval architecture and charming squares, serves as the heart of the coast. Visitors can embark on scenic drives along the winding coastal roads, stopping at enchanting towns like Positano, Ravello, and Sorrento. Additionally, hiking enthusiasts can explore the famous "Path of the Gods" for panoramic views that will leave them in awe.

3.3.3 Sicily:

Located at the tip of Italy's boot, Sicily is the largest island in the Mediterranean Sea and a treasure trove of history, culture, and natural beauty. The island boasts a rich tapestry of influences, from ancient Greek and Roman civilizations to Byzantine, Arab, and Norman influences. Visitors can explore the capital city of Palermo, with its vibrant markets and impressive architecture, including the Palermo Cathedral and the Norman Palace. Discover the awe-inspiring Valley of the Temples in Agrigento, a UNESCO World Heritage Site showcasing well-preserved ancient Greek ruins. Mount Etna, Europe's largest active volcano, offers adventurous travelers the opportunity to hike its slopes and witness its volcanic activity up close.

Throughout Southern Italy, visitors can indulge in the region's renowned culinary delights. Sample authentic Neapolitan cuisine, including delectable pastries like sfogliatelle and iconic dishes such as spaghetti alle vongole (spaghetti with clams). On the Amalfi Coast, savor freshly caught seafood, flavorful limoncello, and the region's famous gelato. In Sicily, treat your taste buds to arancini (fried rice balls), cannoli, and Marsala wine.

To fully embrace the culture of Southern Italy, take part in traditional festivals and events. Naples hosts the vibrant Carnival, featuring colorful parades and masked parties, while Sicily celebrates religious processions and feasts such as the Feast of St. Agatha in Catania.

Traveling through Southern Italy is a journey filled with historical wonders, picturesque landscapes, and unforgettable gastronomic experiences. Whether exploring the vibrant streets of Naples, marveling at the Amalfi Coast's breathtaking beauty, or immersing yourself in Sicily's captivating history, the region promises to leave a lasting impression on every traveler fortunate enough to experience its charm.

Must-See Attractions and Experiences

4.1 Colosseum and Ancient Rome

The Colosseum stands as an iconic symbol of Ancient Rome's grandeur and rich history. This colossal amphitheater, dating back to 70-80 AD, once hosted thrilling gladiatorial battles, theatrical performances, and public spectacles. In this section, we will explore the Colosseum and Ancient Rome, immersing ourselves in the fascinating tales of this historic site.

The Colosseum: Discover the architectural marvel that is the Colosseum, with its imposing structure and ingenious engineering. Learn about its capacity to hold up to 50,000 spectators and the various events that took place within its walls. Explore the underground chambers and maze-like passageways where gladiators prepared for their battles. Marvel at the intricate details of the amphitheater's design and imagine the roar of the crowds that once filled its grand stands.

Roman Forum: Adjacent to the Colosseum lies the Roman Forum, once the heart of ancient Roman political and social life. Delve into the ruins of temples, basilicas, and public squares that once bustled with activity. Walk in the footsteps of emperors as you explore the remnants of the Senate House, the Arch of Septimius Severus, and the Temple of Vesta. Allow your imagination to transport you back in time to an era of power, ambition, and cultural brilliance.

Palatine Hill: Ascend Palatine Hill, the legendary birthplace of Rome, and immerse yourself in the splendor of the imperial palaces that once graced its slopes. Admire the breathtaking views of the Roman Forum below as you wander through the ruins of opulent residences, lush gardens, and sprawling courtyards. Gain insight into the lives of emperors and the opulence of Ancient Rome's elite.

4.2 Vatican City and St. Peter's Basilica

Nestled within the heart of Rome, Vatican City is a sovereign city-state and the spiritual center of Catholicism. Here, we explore the wonders of Vatican City, including St. Peter's Basilica and its awe-inspiring treasures.

St. Peter's Basilica: Marvel at the grandeur of St. Peter's Basilica, one of the world's most significant Christian pilgrimage sites. Admire the sheer size and intricate beauty of this Renaissance masterpiece, designed by renowned architects such as Michelangelo and Bernini. Explore the basilica's interior, adorned with stunning works of art, including Michelangelo's Pietà. Climb to the top of the dome for breathtaking panoramic views of Vatican City and Rome.

Vatican Museums: Immerse yourself in the vast collection of art and historical artifacts housed within the Vatican Museums. Discover masterpieces by legendary artists such as Raphael, Caravaggio, and Leonardo da Vinci. Walk through the mesmerizing Gallery of Maps, the Raphael Rooms, and the magnificent Sistine Chapel, adorned with Michelangelo's awe-inspiring frescoes. Experience the richness of Vatican history and culture as you wander through the halls of this renowned institution.

4.3 The Duomo of Florence and Uffizi Gallery

Florence, the birthplace of the Renaissance, beckons with its artistic wonders and architectural marvels. Two notable attractions in this city steal the spotlight: the magnificent Duomo and the Uffizi Gallery.

The Duomo (Cathedral of Santa Maria del Fiore): Stand in awe of the Duomo, Florence's most iconic landmark. Admire the intricate details of its stunning marble façade and the famous dome engineered by Filippo Brunelleschi. Ascend the dome for panoramic views of the city and take in the beauty of the cathedral's interior, adorned with frescoes

and stained glass windows. Explore the Baptistery of San Giovanni, known for its magnificent bronze doors, and the elegant Giotto's Bell Tower nearby. The Duomo complex is a testament to the architectural and artistic achievements of the Renaissance era.

Uffizi Gallery: Immerse yourself in the artistic treasures housed within the Uffizi Gallery, one of the world's most renowned art museums. Marvel at works by masters such as Botticelli, Michelangelo, Leonardo da Vinci, and Raphael. Admire Botticelli's "The Birth of Venus" and "Primavera," Michelangelo's "Doni Tondo," and Leonardo's "Annunciation." Explore the museum's vast collection, which spans centuries of artistic brilliance, and gain a deeper understanding of the Renaissance's profound impact on art and culture.

4.4 Italian Cuisine and Wine

No journey to Italy is complete without indulging in its world-famous cuisine and wine. Italian gastronomy is a celebration of flavors, fresh ingredients, and time-honored traditions. In this section, we will tantalize your taste buds with a glimpse into the delectable world of Italian food and wine.

Regional Delicacies: Explore the diverse culinary traditions of Italy's regions. From the rich pasta dishes of Emilia-Romagna to the Neapolitan pizza in Naples, each region offers unique and mouthwatering specialties. Sample Tuscan delights such as bistecca alla Fiorentina (Florentine steak) and ribollita (hearty vegetable soup). Indulge in the seafood delicacies of the Amalfi Coast or the aromatic truffle-infused dishes of Piedmont. Let the flavors of Italy take you on a gastronomic journey like no other.

Wine Culture: Italy is renowned for its exceptional wines, and each region boasts its own varietals and vineyards. Discover the world of Italian wine, from the robust reds of Tuscany, such as Chianti and Brunello di Montalcino, to the sparkling wines of Veneto, like Prosecco and Franciacorta. Visit vineyards and wineries to learn about the winemaking process and indulge in tastings that will leave you with a newfound appreciation for Italy's vinicultural heritage.

Culinary Experiences: Immerse yourself in Italian culinary traditions by participating in cooking classes, food tours, and tastings. Learn how to make homemade pasta, traditional pizzas, or creamy gelato from skilled chefs. Visit local markets and sample artisanal cheeses, cured meats, and freshly harvested produce. Engage in the vibrant food culture of Italy, where every meal is a celebration of quality ingredients and time-honored techniques.

4.5 Outdoor Adventures and Nature Parks

Italy's natural beauty extends far beyond its cities and historic sites. The country is home to breathtaking landscapes, stunning coastlines, and picturesque nature parks. In this section, we will explore the outdoor adventures and nature parks that offer a refreshing escape from the urban bustle.

Cinque Terre: Embark on a hike along the rugged coastline of Cinque Terre, a collection of five colorful fishing villages perched on cliffs overlooking the Ligurian Sea. Traverse the scenic trails that connect the villages, passing through vineyards, terraced hillsides, and enchanting coastal vistas.

Dolomites: Discover the majestic beauty of the Dolomites, a mountain range in northeastern Italy. Whether you're an avid hiker, skier, or simply an admirer of breathtaking scenery, the Dolomites offer a range of outdoor activities amidst stunning alpine landscapes, crystal-clear lakes, and charming mountain villages.

Amalfi Coast: Indulge in the coastal beauty of the Amalfi Coast, with its dramatic cliffs, turquoise waters, and picturesque towns. Take leisurely walks along cliffside paths, soak up the sun on stunning beaches, or sail along the coast to explore hidden coves and grottoes.

National Parks: Italy is home to several national parks, each offering its own unique natural wonders. From the rugged peaks of Gran Paradiso National Park to the ancient forests of Abruzzo National Park, nature enthusiasts can engage in hiking, wildlife spotting, and immerse themselves in the country's diverse ecosystems.

Immerse yourself in the splendor of Italy's natural landscapes and engage in outdoor adventures that will leave you with unforgettable memories of the country's breathtaking beauty.

Practical Information and Tips

5.1 Getting Around Italy

Navigating Italy's diverse cities and picturesque countryside can be an exciting part of your journey. Here are some practical tips on getting around in Italy:

a. Public Transportation:

Italy boasts an extensive and efficient public transportation network, including trains, buses, and metros. The national train service, Trenitalia, offers reliable connections between major cities and towns.

Rome, Milan, and Naples have extensive metro systems, while buses are a common mode of transport in smaller towns. Purchase tickets in advance or at designated ticket booths or machines before boarding.

b. Renting a Car:

If you plan to explore Italy's countryside or smaller towns, renting a car can provide flexibility and convenience. International driving permits are recommended, along with a valid driver's license from your home country.

Be prepared for narrow, winding roads, especially in rural areas. Familiarize yourself with local driving rules and regulations, and consider booking parking spaces in advance, especially in major cities.

c. Taxis and Ridesharing:

Taxis are readily available in Italian cities, but they can be expensive. Make sure the taxi is licensed, and insist on using the meter or agreeing on a fare before starting the journey.

Ridesharing services like Uber and Lyft operate in major cities, providing an alternative and often more cost-effective means of transportation. Check the availability and pricing in your desired location.

d. Cycling and Walking:

Italy's cities and towns are often best explored on foot or by bicycle. Many cities offer bike rental services, and there are dedicated cycling paths in certain areas.

Walking is a great way to soak in the charm of Italian streets and neighborhoods. Keep in mind that Italian cities are known for their cobblestone streets, so wear comfortable footwear.

5.2 Accommodation Options

Italy offers a wide range of accommodation options to suit various budgets and preferences. Here are some popular choices:

a. Hotels:

From luxury hotels to boutique establishments and budget-friendly options, Italy has a diverse hotel scene. Major cities and tourist hotspots have a plethora of choices. Consider the location, amenities, and customer reviews when making a selection.

b. Bed and Breakfast (B&B) and Guesthouses:

B&Bs and guesthouses offer a more intimate and personalized experience. They are often family-run establishments, providing cozy rooms and a home-like atmosphere. These options are particularly popular in smaller towns and rural areas.

c. Agriturismo:

Agriturismo refers to farm stays, where visitors can experience rural life and enjoy local produce. These accommodations range from rustic farmhouses to elegant country estates. Agriturismo is an excellent choice for those seeking a tranquil and immersive experience.

d. Vacation Rentals:

Italy has a thriving vacation rental market, with apartments, villas, and holiday homes available for short-term stays. Websites like Airbnb and HomeAway offer a wide selection of properties, allowing you to live like a local and enjoy more space and privacy.

e. Hostels:

Ideal for budget-conscious travelers, hostels provide affordable shared or private rooms. They often offer communal areas, kitchen facilities, and opportunities to meet fellow travelers. Hostels are popular in major cities and backpacker destinations.

f. Monasteries and Convents:

For a unique and spiritual experience, some monasteries and convents in Italy offer accommodation to travelers. These establishments provide a peaceful and reflective environment, often located in scenic surroundings.

When selecting accommodation, consider factors such as location, proximity to attractions or public transportation, safety, and the overall ambiance that aligns with your travel preferences.

Remember to book well in advance, especially during peak tourist seasons, to secure your desired accommodation and take advantage of any early bird discounts.

g. Reservations and Booking:

It is advisable to make reservations for your accommodation in advance, especially during peak tourist seasons or if you have specific preferences. This ensures availability and allows you to secure the best rates.

Consider using reputable booking websites or contacting accommodations directly to make reservations. Read reviews from previous guests to get an idea of the quality and service provided.

h. Location:

When choosing your accommodation, consider its location in relation to your planned activities and attractions. Staying in the city center may provide easy access to landmarks, restaurants, and nightlife, while accommodations in quieter neighborhoods or outskirts can offer a more relaxed atmosphere.

i. Safety and Security:

Prioritize safety when selecting accommodation. Look for properties with good security measures, such as 24-hour reception, secure entrances, and in-room safes for storing valuables.

Read reviews or ask about the safety of the surrounding neighborhood, particularly if you plan to walk around at night. Trust your instincts and take necessary precautions to ensure a secure stay.

j. Amenities and Facilities:

Consider the amenities and facilities offered by the accommodation. This may include free Wi-Fi, breakfast options, air conditioning, laundry services, fitness centers, swimming pools, or on-site restaurants.

Determine which amenities are essential to you and choose accordingly to enhance your comfort and convenience during your stay.

k. Language and Communication:

While many accommodations in popular tourist areas have staff who speak English, it's always helpful to learn a few basic Italian phrases or carry a translation app to communicate effectively.

If you have specific requests or requirements, such as dietary restrictions or accessibility needs, communicate them clearly to the accommodation provider before your arrival to ensure a smooth experience.

l. Check-in and Check-out:

Familiarize yourself with the check-in and check-out times of your chosen accommodation. If you have early or late arrival/departure times, contact the property in advance to arrange for any necessary accommodations or luggage storage options.

m. Local Taxes and Fees:

Some accommodations may charge additional local taxes or fees that are not included in the initial booking price. Clarify the total cost and inquire about any additional charges to avoid surprises during check-out.

n. Responsible Tourism:

Consider staying at accommodations that prioritize sustainable practices and responsible tourism. Look for eco-friendly certifications, waste reduction initiatives, and support for local communities to contribute positively to the destinations you visit.

Remember, each accommodation option has its own unique characteristics and advantages. Research, plan, and choose based on your personal preferences, budget, and desired travel experience. By selecting the right accommodation, you can enhance your overall trip to Italy and ensure a comfortable and enjoyable stay.

6.1 Essential Italian Phrases

Learning a few essential Italian phrases can greatly enhance your travel experience in Italy, allowing you to connect with locals and navigate daily interactions more smoothly. Here are some key phrases to help you communicate effectively:

Greetings and Basic Expressions:

Ciao (chow) - Hello/Goodbye (informal)

Buongiorno (bwon-JOR-no) - Good morning/Good day

Buonasera (bwoh-nah-SAY-rah) - Good evening

Grazie (GRAH-tsee-eh) - Thank you

Prego (PREH-goh) - You're welcome/Please

Mi scusi (mee SKOO-zee) - Excuse me

Per favore (pehr fah-VOH-reh) - Please

Mi dispiace (mee dee-SPYA-cheh) - I'm sorry

Introductions and Polite Phrases:

Come ti chiami? (koh-meh tee KYAH-mee) - What is your name?

Mi chiamo... (mee KYAH-moh) - My name is...

Piacere di conoscerti (pee-AH-cheh-reh dee koh-noh-SHER-tee) - Nice to meet you

Scusa, parli inglese? (SKOO-zah, PAR-lee een-GLEH-zeh) - Excuse me, do you speak English?

Non capisco (non kah-PEES-koh) - I don't understand

Ordering Food and Drinks:

Vorrei... (vor-RAY) - I would like...

Un tavolo per uno/due, per favore (oon tah-VOH-lo pehr OO-no/DOO-eh, pehr fah-VOH-reh) - A table for one/two, please

Il conto, per favore (eel KON-to, pehr fah-VOH-reh) - The bill, please

Mi piacerebbe provare questo (mee pee-ah-cheh-REB-beh proh-VAH-reh KWEH-stoh) - I would like to try this

Asking for Directions:

Dov'è...? (doh-VEH) - Where is...?

A sinistra (ah see-NEES-trah) - To the left

A destra (ah DEH-strah) - To the right

Avanti (ah-VAHN-tee) - Straight ahead

Scusi, può aiutarmi? (SKOO-zee, pwoh ah-YOO-tar-mee) - Excuse me, can you help me?

Quanto dista...? (KWAHN-toh DEES-tah) - How far is...?

Numbers and Counting:

Uno (OO-no) - One

Due (DOO-eh) - Two

Tre (TREH) - Three

Dieci (DEE-eh-chee) - Ten

Cento (CHEN-toh) - One hundred

Mille (MEEL-leh) - One thousand

Remember, practicing these phrases with confidence and a friendly attitude will go a long way in fostering positive interactions with locals and immersing yourself in the Italian culture.

6.2 Italian Alphabet and Pronunciation Guide

The Italian alphabet consists of 21 letters, including five vowels (a, e, i, o, u) and 16 consonants. Understanding the correct pronunciation of each letter will help you communicate effectively in Italian. Here is a guide to the Italian alphabet and its approximate pronunciation:

A (ah) - like "ah" in "father"

B (bee) - like "b" in "boy"

C (chee) - like "k" in "kite" before a, o, u; like "ch" in "cheese" before e, i

D (dee) - like "d" in "dog"

E (eh) - like "e" in "bed"

F (effe) - like "f" in "fox"

G (gee) - like "g" in "go" before a, o, u; like "j" in "jump" before e, i

H (acca) - silent in most words

I (ee) - like "ee" in "see"

L (elle) - like "l" in "love"

M (emme) - like "m" in "mother"

N (enne) - like "n" in "no"

O (oh) - like "o" in "more"

P (pee) - like "p" in "pen"

Q (ku) - always followed by "u" and pronounced like "kw" in "queen"

R (erre) - rolled "r" sound

S (esse) - like "s" in "sun"

T (tee) - like "t" in "top"

U (oo) - like "oo" in "moon"

V (vu) - like "v" in "victory"

Z (zeta) - like "z" in "zoo"

By familiarizing yourself with the Italian alphabet and its pronunciation, you will be better equipped to read signs, menus, and other written materials during your travels in Italy. Practice speaking the letters aloud to refine your pronunciation and enhance your language skills.

Conclusion and Final Recommendations

As your journey through Italy comes to an end, it is time to reflect on the experiences, sights, and memories that have shaped your adventure. The "Italy Travel Guide 2023" has been your trusted companion, providing valuable insights and practical information that have enhanced your exploration of this captivating country. In this concluding chapter, we summarize the highlights of your journey and offer final recommendations for making the most of your time in Italy.

Throughout your travels, you have immersed yourself in Italy's rich history, culture, and natural beauty. From the ancient ruins of Rome to the Renaissance art in Florence, and the charming canals of Venice, each city and region has offered a unique tapestry of experiences. You have marveled at iconic landmarks, indulged in mouthwatering cuisine, and connected with the warm and hospitable locals who have made your stay memorable.

As you reflect on your time in Italy, consider the following final recommendations:

Embrace the Slow Pace of Italian Life: Italy is known for its "dolce vita" or sweet life. Take the time to savor each moment, whether it's enjoying a leisurely meal, strolling through charming streets, or simply sitting in a piazza with a cup of coffee. Embrace the laid-back lifestyle and immerse yourself in the vibrant atmosphere that surrounds you.

Explore Beyond the Tourist Hotspots: While Rome, Florence, and Venice are undoubtedly captivating, consider venturing off the beaten path to discover Italy's hidden gems. Visit smaller towns and villages such as Siena, Lucca, or Assisi, where you can experience a more authentic and intimate side of Italian life.

Interact with the Locals: Italians are known for their warmth and friendliness. Strike up conversations with locals, learn a few basic Italian phrases, and embrace the opportunity to connect with the people you meet along the way. Their insights and recommendations can lead to unexpected adventures and create lasting memories.

Immerse Yourself in Italian Cuisine: Italy is a paradise for food lovers, and no trip is complete without indulging in its culinary delights. Sample regional specialties, visit local markets, and consider taking a cooking class to learn the art of creating authentic

Italian dishes. Don't forget to pair your meals with local wines, which vary in flavor and character across different regions.

Take Time to Wander: While it's important to have an itinerary, leave room for serendipity. Allow yourself to get lost in the winding streets, stumble upon hidden squares, and stumble upon unexpected treasures. Some of the most memorable experiences can come from embracing spontaneity and following your instincts.

Preserve Italy's Cultural Heritage: Italy's historical and artistic heritage is unparalleled. As you visit museums, galleries, and historical sites, respect the rules and regulations in place to preserve these treasures. Avoid touching artwork, follow photography guidelines, and be mindful of the importance of preserving Italy's cultural legacy for future generations.

Share Your Italian Journey: As your adventure in Italy comes to an end, share your experiences and stories with others. Inspire fellow travelers, friends, and family to discover the beauty and magic of Italy. Share your photos, write about your favorite moments, and spread the joy that this country has brought to your life.

In conclusion, the "Italy Travel Guide 2023" has served as a valuable resource, empowering you to navigate Italy's diverse regions, historical landmarks, and cultural wonders. It has provided you with the tools to craft an unforgettable journey, allowing you to immerse yourself in Italy's vibrant tapestry of art, history, cuisine, and natural beauty.

As you bid farewell to Italy, cherish the memories you have created and carry the spirit of this remarkable country with you. Remember that Italy will always welcome you back with open arms, ready to unveil new experiences and hidden treasures. And as you continue your travels, may the lessons learned and the joy discovered in Italy inspire your future adventures.

Arrivederci e buon viaggio! (Goodbye and safe travels!)

BONUS

TRAVEL JOURNAL

DAY	EXPERIENCE
1	
2	
3	
4	
5	
6	
7	

8	
9	
10	
11	
12	
13	
14	
15	
16	
17	
18	

19	
20	
21	

Dear Reader,

As you embark on new journeys and adventures, I want to send you a heartfelt message of good luck. May your path be filled with excitement, joy, and discovery.

May you find courage to step out of your comfort zone and embrace new experiences. May you have the strength to overcome challenges and the resilience to bounce back from setbacks. Remember that every obstacle is an opportunity for growth and learning.

May you encounter kind souls along the way who will inspire and uplift you. May you create lasting memories and forge meaningful connections with the people you meet. Open your heart to the beauty of diversity and let it enrich your journey.

May you have moments of awe as you witness the wonders of the world. From breathtaking landscapes to architectural marvels, let them remind you of the magnificence of our planet. Take the time to appreciate the simple pleasures and find beauty in the ordinary.

May you be guided by intuition and serendipity, allowing unexpected detours to lead you to extraordinary experiences. Trust in your instincts and have faith in your ability to navigate through life's twists and turns.

Remember that the true essence of travel lies not only in the destinations you reach, but in the transformation that happens within you. Allow each adventure to shape and inspire you, leaving an indelible mark on your soul.

So, as you set forth on your path, may luck be your faithful companion. May it bring you opportunities, happiness, and a sense of fulfillment. May it guide you towards the experiences that will bring you the greatest joy.

Believe in yourself and your dreams, for you are capable of achieving greatness. Embrace the unknown with enthusiasm and embrace the challenges with resilience. The world is vast, and it eagerly awaits your exploration.

Safe Travels!